Praise for Teen Secrets

One of the 50 Best Books for Teens and Tweens!
RadicalParenting.Com

Lori Hanson has taken a tough subject head on and has made it easy for anyone to know exactly what to do to WIN a battle with bulimia. After 34 years of experience, she has walked her talk and can help your students like few others can.

Jonathan Sprinkles,
Former National College Speaker of the Year, APCA
www.JSprinkles.com

I just finished this book and loved it! It is so easy to read and understand, great for both parents and teens to read. Award-winning author Lori Hanson did a great job at getting across serious issues in a positive and encouraging fashion that teens reading this will feel like she "gets them". I love the incorporation of The Secret, *visualization, and the vision board!*

What is fantastic is that teens have a limited attention span when it comes to reading books and Lori put this in an abbreviated format that is deep in understanding, totally encouraging and beneficial for both parents and teens alike.

Sue Scheff, Author, Wit's End, Founder P.U.R.E.
(Parent's Universal Resource Expert)
SueScheff.blogspot.com

In Teen Secrets to Surviving & THRIVING *award-winning author, speaker and consultant Lori Hanson draws upon a depth of personal experience, expertise and wisdom to empower teens in a frank and fun way. Her five valuable life principles are comfort brain and spirit food for the teen in your life—they'll gobble them up!*
BARB BEST, BarbBest.com & BBevHills.com

What teens are saying:
This book helped me through a very difficult time in my life. It also helped me realize I'm definitely not alone when it comes to insecurity, and all the other feelings being a teen gives us!
—Elle S., age 13

It really made me realize that I can get through something that I am going through right now and that no matter what my happiness is more important and that I am going to be okay.
—Kiana, age 20

I liked how she told her life story and made it into a positive outlet. It made me realize a couple things that I tend to do relating to her.
—Adriana R., age 19

I enjoyed how she expressed new ways for me to handle either anger or frustration. She has over come a lot and I am inspired by it.
—Matthew G., age 19

Everything was cool. I liked the Metal of Honor Card part. That's a happy card.
—Paul, age 18

What I like most about Lori's message was that she didn't give up and did something good with her life.
—Alexis M., Age 14

Teen Secrets

to

Surviving &
THRIVING

*How to Deal with Stress,
Be Confident and Feel Great*

This book is brought to you by:
Suel & Associates
Family Therapy, Hypnotherapy

Teen Secrets
to
Surviving &
THRIVING

How to Deal with Stress,
Be Confident and Feel Great

Lori Hanson

25379 Wayne Mills Place, Suite 228
Valencia, CA 91355
www.ShewolfPress.com

PUBLISHED BY: Shewolf Press
                  25379 Wayne Mills Pl. #228, Valencia, CA 91355
                  www.ShewolfPress.com

Cover design by Kendra Kellogg, nz graphics
Interior design by WESType Publishing Services, Inc., Boulder, Colorado

First Edition.

ISBN: 978-0-9800128-2-8

Printed and bound in the USA

    10 9 8 7 6 5 4 3 2 1 0

Books may be purchased in quantity and/or special sales by contacting the publisher, Shewolf Press, at 25379 Wayne Mills Place, Suite 228, Valencia, CA 91355, 877-650-HEAL or through the website, ShewolfPress.com.

This book is printed on acid-free paper.

This book is dedicated to teens everywhere who struggle to find their identity; fit in; measure up; be cool, confident and successful; and feel like they belong on this planet...in this lifetime. May this book offer hope, inspiration, laughter and encouragement to continue on your path each day and know there is a place where YOU fit into this puzzle called teenage life. A place where you will feel special, know you belong and are important just because you are!

Table of Contents

Foreword

Teens today are stressed out. Life is moving at a faster pace everyday with increasing pressure to perform, fit in and excel. The number of teens who turn to drugs, alcohol, eating disorders and violence to deal with this stress is staggering. They are getting addicted earlier, faster and harder than ever before.

Teens are growing up on a fast running treadmill, and often can't find the switch to slow it down or turn it off and catch their breath. In a world dominated by technology they communicate through cell phones, social media and text messaging and rarely shut down.

Being a teenager has never been easy, but today's teens have more pressure, more stress, and less quality family time than ever before. Without coping skills they are at risk of adopting addictive behaviors at an early age that will significantly affect their quality of life and ability to achieve their dreams.

Lori Hanson has a passion for helping teens navigate the maze of adolescence to adulthood. When she was a teen Lori was consumed with peer pressure, media pressure, insecurities and low self-esteem. At fourteen she found a coping mechanism through food, a pattern that continued in her life for over thirty years.

Lori realized that what she learned in her recovery from bulimia was a gift she had to share. After a successful twenty-eight year career in corporate America, she left to dedicate her time talking to teens and college students to give them tools for improving self-esteem, dealing with peer pressure, stress and anger. She's also on a mission to increase awareness about eating disorders, addictive behaviors and the importance of diet and nutrition as a foundation to overall success in life.

When you meet Lori you are immediately struck by her passion for helping kids. Her intent and spirit is genuine and they feel the connection when she speaks to them. Teens love her openness, approachability, willingness to laugh at herself and be one of the them. Teens thank her for sharing her life story and making it a positive outlet they can learn from. They tell her how much she has inspired them to live a better life; understanding and utilizing the tools she shares, they know they can get through anything.

This book includes the five Hot Pastry Principles™ Lori developed and shares in speeches, consultations and workshops. Packed full of great advice that's easy to digest, this book covers all the hot topics for teens. How to cope with stress, why it's important to like yourself, understanding how your thoughts affect your life, why diet and nutrition matter even if you're thin, and why it's important to slow down, stay centered and continually improve your mental and physical health.

Wisely packaged in a short format, this book is perfect for teens with short attention spans. Full of great stories, humor and illustrations, the Hot Pastry Principles are the keys to happiness, success, appreciating and loving your life. This book is a must read for every teen!

James Malinchak
Contributing Author,
Chicken Soup for the Teenage Soul
Co-Author, *Chicken Soup for the College Soul*
Author, *Teenagers Tips for Success*
www.Malinchak.com

Acknowledgments

I am fortunate to be surrounded by a talented and knowledgeable team of people from the independent publishing community who supported me and helped me create this book.

Mara Purl thanks for providing vision, inspiration, guidance, and the gift of friendship. Having you take an interest in my projects has not only helped me breathe life into them, but market them with genius. Your generosity in connecting me with what and who you know is most appreciated. You are an angel.

Barb Munson you are the best! Your editing is impeccable and working with you is easy. Thanks for doing your part to help this book come to life quickly. You are my rudder always keeping me headed in the right direction. Your enthusiasm and expertise helped make this process a delight.

Ronnie Moore a sincere thank you for creating another beautifully designed book. Your enthusiasm for my projects always shines though.

Acknowledgments

Thanks to Kendra Kellogg for working diligently to understand my concept and create the artwork for the cover. You were a joy to work with.

Nick Zelinger thanks for jumping in at the last minute to finalize the cover design and pull this all together.

Judith Briles your guidance and mentoring has been invaluable. Thank you for continuing to provide the best resources and knowledge just when I need it.

A very special thanks to my nieces and nephews without whom this book would not exist. Lace, DJ, Evan, Tayler, Justin and Vincent. Having you in my life keeps me young and gives me that much needed outlet to be silly and connect with my inner kid. You guys rock!

Introduction

You don't know me, but I've been called all kinds of names in my life. "Dogface" was one of my favorites (okay, not really a fave), but there was a time in middle school when I walked down the hall and the guys who sat next to me in band barked, laughed and said, "Hey, there's Dog face!" I never was a cheerleader but I certainly wasn't butt-ugly either. Despite my lack of self-confidence I knew I didn't deserve *that* title. I've been called "cute" when what I really wanted was to be beautiful, and I've been appreciated by people I hoped *wouldn't* notice me and ignored by those I longed to connect with.

I spent many years trying to figure out where I fit in. 'Cos I never really felt like I did. I attended five schools between first and twelfth grades. That made it kind of hard to make long-lasting friendships and feel like I really belonged. My teen years were the pits—a time filled with a desire to fit in with the jocks combined with a need to be independent, a desperate need to get my parents (specifically my mom) off my back and a chronic feeling that I couldn't breathe because of all the control in my life.

This all led me to an eating disorder that started at the age of fourteen. I could have gone in many directions but eating worked for me. So what that meant was I began to use food to deal with anything that made me uncomfortable. Incredibly I continued this behavior until I was in my forties!

I suffered from bulimia. But before you say, "Eeeewww! She ate and threw up," let me share with you that not all bulimics purge. There are two types of bulimics, purging and non-purging. Dr. Ira Sacker addresses this is his book, *Regaining Your Self* Hyperion, 2007. Many people with bulimia eat horrific amounts of food and then use excessive exercise, laxatives, diet pills or strict diets (my choice) to control the weight gain.

I had a rough transition to adulthood and, judging by the scores of teens who develop eating disorders and drug and alcohol addiction, I know I'm not the only one. So many teens haven't figured out to deal with stress we now have organizations like Stressed Out Students. Some kids pull out a gun and massacre students at their school because they feel they don't fit in, or maybe somebody bullied them or made them feel stupid and unwanted. I lived ten minutes from Columbine High School when *that* shooting rampage happened.

I think it's so incredibly sad that we exist day after day and don't even know how much someone else is hurting. I've said this many times: it's amazing any of us grow up because kids are so mean to each other! But somehow we get through. We survive the cruelty of bullies and kids that cut us down or make fun of us just to make themselves feel better, cooler, mightier. We even manage to have some fun and enjoy our teen years a bit.

I am truly blessed to have two teenage nieces and four teenage nephews who enjoy hanging out with me and have since they were young. With four of them I'm known as the "Ice Cream Aunt." We had an annual tradition for many years of "Cookie Night" before Christmas when we baked and decorated cookies and watched *The Grinch Who Stole Christmas*. I also would take them to Mile High Nationals (NHRA drag races) every summer in the foothills above Denver. And we've done plenty of sleepovers.

I became known as the "Crazy Aunt" when I had my red Nissan King Cab pickup truck (complete with a roll bar and lights) and they giggled with delight as they begged me to drive faster to pass other cars (they were three and four years old at the time). That was fun until I got my first red sports car when they were teens and we took the "favorite 100 mph on-ramp." Now that was fun!

Through my nieces and nephews I've been able to stay young, act crazy and stay connected even now. I've learned a lot about the Internet from watching them and they've learned a thing or two from me. Just recently, my niece Tayler even helped me set up my MySpace page.

After writing my first book about my recovery from bulimia, I left Corporate America (my day job) and started speaking to teens and college kids about self-esteem, body image, peer pressure and how to live a happier life while transitioning through your teens.

My goal is to help teens develop a tool set of coping mechanisms to avoid addictive behaviors. Well—honestly my goal is to help you figure out how to be happy in life much sooner than I did. I lived for over thirty years obsessed with what I saw in the mirror and what other people thought of me. Then one day I woke up and realized people weren't nearly as tuned into me as I thought they were! I had the responsibility to love and accept myself and once I did I saw that people responded to me differently. I didn't have to work at being "cool, hip or fly." When I got comfortable being "me" I was able to attract cool, supportive people into my life. And ignore those who didn't get me, because I don't need mean, unsupportive people in my life.

As teens you are growing up in a world much different than I did. There is much more fear, worry and crime directed at teens. At ten years old I stayed home alone to babysit my little brother. I played outside and no one worried that I might be kidnapped.

There weren't home computers or cell phones; I played outside, rode my bike, jumped rope and rode our horse. Times are different and the world has evolved. I'm sure you can't imagine life without your cell phones or computers.

So where do you get the information you need to be happy these days? Most teens I know don't want to listen to their parents, teachers or anyone of authority. That's how I was—rebellious! Or maybe you do want to listen but can't get your parents to tune in long enough to give you good advice. How do you find your way through the trek of adolescence as a well adjusted, happy kid in a state where you can not only survive, but thrive in your teenage years?

In this book you'll find Hot Pastry Principles™, developed from twenty-five years of studying self-esteem, diet, health, nutrition and the power of the subconscious. It is my hope that through these principles, along with some great stories and humor, I'll be able to motivate and inspire you to live life with passion, confidence, laughter and the knowledge that you can achieve *anything* and *everything* you desire in this life! Because you can.

—Lori Hanson

Chapter One

❧

It Started
With Pop–Tarts®

I t's almost midnight. I'm sitting on the couch, drowsy after yet another food-induced stupor. I have a big test at school tomorrow and I can hardly breathe, I ate so much. There's no way I will be able to sleep tonight.

This is SO stupid! I did it again. What is wrong with me!?

The pressures of life have once again driven me to my place of personal solace. Well, actually it's more of a personal numbness, but it's the place I run to when…

- ✧ I feel left out
- ✧ I'm drowning, stressed out with my studies, sports, and other activities
- ✧ I'm lonely
- ✧ I'm frustrated
- ✧ I'm scared, depressed, worried

- ✧ No one understands me
- ✧ I'm angry
- ✧ I hate my body
- ✧ I want to scream and can't
- ✧ All I want to do is cry
- ✧ I don't want to feel

This is a wickedly vicious cycle, and one I have perfected.

Tonight? A large four-cheese pizza, with bread sticks; a half bag of nachos, a half-gallon of Baskin-Robbins Pralines 'n Cream ice cream and half a bag of Oreos. Caught in the realization I had fallen again, the unhealthy internal dialogue in my head was set to warp speed.

I was just getting myself back on track and feeling better, and here I am again. Why do I do this? Why can't I control it? Why is there no way to stop myself from the frenzied need to eat until I can't move? I hate myself! I'm so miserable I could scream! Tomorrow I will be all swollen; my clothes will be tight. Everyone will all see how big my stomach looks. I will be so embarrassed.

…It's morning. I hear the alarm clock. I'm so groggy that it's all I can to do to coax myself out of bed.

I'm going to be late! I don't want to move. I don't want to get dressed. I want to hibernate. I can't pos-

sibly face the world outside today. That's it…tonight when I come home, I will eat healthy. No more sweets!

Three weeks have passed. It's time to weigh and measure like I do *every* Sunday. I made some progress since my last slide. My clothes are starting to feel looser and I feel my energy starting to return. It's been a good couple of weeks and this time I think I'm on track. I can win this battle. The next time I get upset I just won't eat, I promise; I will be strong. I won't let food get the better of me.

Well, let me back up and tell you how it all started. I was an early inductee into the sugar "hall of fame." Food was associated with family celebrations, social get-togethers, Saturday nights spent at friends' homes and holidays. Food was *central* to life.

Many childhood issues helped form my self-destructive behavior. As I reached the adolescent years, my interest in boys, combined with a poor self-image and lack of confidence in myself, sent me to the safe haven of bulimia.

My bulimia started at 14, my first year away from home at boarding school. A friend who worked in the cafeteria and I ripped off an industrial size bag of Pop-Tarts® Toaster Pastries and brought them back to our room. I came back to the room one day feeling really down and discovered that eating a Pop-Tarts® made me feel better. I didn't realize at the time it was the sugar rush that did it. But as I ate a second and third, I was able to create a nice little numb haven that seemed to dim the pain of the world from my consciousness.

My bulimia was at its worst during college and the first few years of my career. By that time, it was a chronic cycle of bingeing to excess, followed by religious dieting and starving myself for weeks to compensate. As a person who abuses food, you do so many embarrassing things. Things you never tell anyone else about!

All I wanted was to feel a distance from the world, to achieve the state of numbness where I didn't care about anyone or anything. I was just a huge screw up! I couldn't control my food intake, I didn't look like other girls whom I thought were attractive; and I certainly didn't look like the tall, thin women with big boobs (aka Barbie® doll figures) that most of the guys I knew liked. I was short, muscular and had curvy hips. I didn't fit the mold, didn't measure up.

This was the message I picked up from my childhood and teen years. I didn't make straight A's, every time I tried out for the gymnastics team I wasn't good enough, I played violin well and was in a youth orchestra but that just made me *weird* in other kids' eyes. By the time I went to boarding school my motto was "Rules are made to be broken." I was a little hellion and very proud of it. I got kicked out of boarding school twice!

Most of my friends were older than I was and I found the one thing I was good at as a teenager was work. It sure wasn't school! I would read all my chapters using a highlighter and when I was done had no clue what I had just read. I had a lot of trouble staying focused and being "in the moment" of what I was doing.

I was boy crazy from a very early age. In my teens guys became one of my obsessions. But I never dated anyone for very long—when you don't have much confidence in yourself it's difficult to attract guys that treat you well, and if you do, they don't stay around long. Once they see your insecurities they usually run. I would spend hours wondering what I had done that made a guy disappear. What a waste of time that was!

I think the biggest regret I have from my teen years is that I spread myself so thin. I played piano because Mom said I had to; I sang because I had a good voice and enjoyed performing; I played violin because I enjoyed it; I played saxophone because it's the instrument my dad played and I wanted to be like my dad. Need I mention that all of these involved lots of hours of practice!

But what *I* wanted to do was play tennis. At the risk of sounding old (I would say "dating myself" but then you would think I'm really weird!) when I was young, girls weren't nearly as active in sports as they are now. Nobody played soccer where I grew up and parents didn't take girls to play softball or football…yeah, "back in my day" it was different.

The other thing I wish I had done different as a teen is communicated what I needed and wanted to my parents and teachers. But I didn't realize I had to do that, or that they would listen. I existed as a frustrated teen thinking no one really understood me or wanted to. No one "got" me and everyone was out to "get" me, that is, tell on me, get me in trouble, etc.

I had my first cigarette at age eleven, started drinking Strawberry Boone's Farm wine in eighth grade and had my first toke of pot shortly after. I joked about being a wino throughout high school and was drunk off my ass at my high school graduation. I was a wild child heavily influenced by what other people thought of me and my perception of what I thought was cool. Yet, I managed to retain a great sense of humor and quick wit.

Fortunately I never took up smoking. See the problem is, you start something when you're young (like smoking) because it looks so cool and you're being such a rebel doing it! And the next thing you know you're addicted and can't stop. And some of these habits get expensive.

I lost my virginity at seventeen to a guy I was dating who didn't call for a month afterwards. Talk about feeling stupid! Plus, I had been warned—it was my best friend's cousin and she told me not to sleep with him because he would just add me to the list. Live and learn.

I know many teens today are sexually active, but seriously there isn't any rush! You have plenty of time. And sex really is much more rewarding when you are in love and have a true connection with someone. To guys and girls it is a completely different experience as a teen. But we'll get back to this topic.

So I have a colorful past, but it was my path. I'm still in love with the idea of being a rebel, but it was calmed to a degree during my twenty-eight years of being a "successful career woman." Now I have to remind myself to cut loose, be silly and not be afraid to let other people see the "authentic" me. (And now that I live in Southern California where lots of people work hard to hide whom they really are!) I have two incredible dogs that are great at keeping me in touch with my "inner teen."

Now that you know a little about me and my history, let's get on to the good stuff. Here come the Hot Pastry Principles, the secrets for surviving and thriving in your teens!

Don't be afraid to look foolish, it will endear you to others!

The Hot Pastry Principles

Chapter 2

❧

You Gotta Like Yourself!

Principle #1 Maintain Healthy Self-Esteem

So many issues that evolve in life start in our teens. Depending on your upbringing, you may have a really great sense of self-worth and know how you fit in. You may also have a great group of friends who you can always count on to support you and truly understand you.

But if you didn't get a lot of love, support and much needed attention as a kid you may have evolved into an angry, irritable, unhappy teen. You may not feel you fit in anywhere. And you cover it up by acting like it doesn't really matter. You may be a bully, always picking on other kids to show how much better you are.

Or maybe you always put down other kids and make fun of them. Of course you make other kids laugh, but did you know this just shows how insecure you are? I hate to burst your bubble, but being a bully, making fun of other kids and acting superior waves a big red flag that you aren't "all that." And I don't know about you, but I believe in karma…what you throw out in life you will get back. So be careful what you say or do because it *will* come back at you.

How does this happen? How do teens evolve into places that make them act out like they are all that? It happens at a very early age. Our self-esteem is shaped by the time we are five years old. When you are a baby you aren't insecure, self-conscious or paranoid and you don't pick on other people! You know how to ask for exactly what you want and you don't hold back because of what other people might think. If your diapers are wet, you cry; if you're hungry, you cry; if you're happy, you giggle and smile. You communicate your needs perfectly.

But as you start to crawl, walk and explore your world the "rules" come in. Your parents tell you, "Don't touch that," "Don't do that," "Don't say that," "Don't do it that way, do it this way," etc.

As you enter kindergarten and grade school there are more adults in your life telling you what to do and what not to do. If you go to church you're taught what is "right and wrong" by your teachers or pastors at church. So now you've collected a bunch of rules to live by. And what do you do when some of the rules don't make sense? Depending on the level of self-esteem or self-worth you have you'll

Illustration by Lace Hanson

Remind You of Anyone You Know?

respond differently and begin to express your opinions or hold them inside and thus the confusion or conflict begins.

Self–Esteem

So what is self-esteem and how do you know if yours is low? Our self-esteem is made up of several components:

- ✧ **Identity**—A sense of individuality and self. "Who I am." What defines you and your essential character? (Not your role as son, daughter, student, athlete or musician.)
- ✧ **Pride**—You have a realistic sense of your self-respect and worth, you appreciate your achievements, and are thankful for your talents.
- ✧ **Self-Confidence**—Acceptance and belief in your abilities (what you're good at). As your ability or competence increases (playing guitar, piano, soccer, football, gymnastics) your confidence increases.
- ✧ **Accept**—Self-acceptance is belief in and accepting yourself positively. You have identified your weaknesses, but love yourself in spite of them and know you can improve.

✧ **Humility**—You recognize your imperfections or weaknesses, are not arrogant and are conscious of your shortcomings and ignorance but teachable. You understand that we are all valuable.
✧ **Appreciation**—Have a healthy estimate of your quality and worth.

Signs of Low Self-Esteem

Here are a few signs of low self-esteem:

✧ Watching too much TV, vegging out, no energy or drive
✧ Constantly listening to iPod, texting or listening to radio (never alone with your thoughts)
✧ Eating too much, being overweight
✧ Obsession with how you look, constantly comparing yourself to others, embarrassed about your body
✧ Being a bully, being mean to everyone, always picking on other kids
✧ Over-commitment—inability to say "no" or set boundaries
✧ Always late for school, work or appointments
✧ Poor grades or poor performance at work or on your household chores

- ✧ Messy room—lack of pride in yourself and surroundings
- ✧ Negative self-talk (beating yourself up: "I'm fat," "I'm ugly," "No one will ever like me," "I wish I looked like him or her, then people would like me")
- ✧ Self-doubt—thoughts like "I can't do anything right" or "No one understands me or likes me"
- ✧ Sensitive to criticism, unable to take constructive criticism and improve
- ✧ Promiscuity—being sexually active with many partners on a regular basis
- ✧ Depression, isolation, loneliness
- ✧ Eating disorders, drug or alcohol abuse—numbing out from life

Because of the "conditioning" you get growing up from all the "no's," "don't do that," "don't act that way, do it this way" you eventually develop filters and perceptions of how you view the world. Some kids have a strong belief in their abilities (for example, as a student or athlete) while others think they are incapable of having anything they want and therefore are failures.

The issue is whatever you believe is true. As Henry Ford said many years ago, "Whether you think you can or think you can't, you're right!" We'll talk more about our internal belief systems in a little bit.

Ways to Improve Your Self-Esteem

In order to improve your self-esteem you've got to figure out how to feel better about yourself, how to like, accept and, yes—even love yourself!

Communication—Creating YourSpace

You've got to figure out to communicate effectively with people so they understand what's not acceptable to you. This is one thing I sure didn't understand as a teen! I didn't give myself permission to let others know when what they said hurt my feelings. And I wasn't secure enough in myself to break off with a guy that stood me up for a date. I was so desperate to be accepted that I put up with terrible treatment from guys. I let them make fun of me, put me down and berate me in front of other people. I've got great news for both girls and guys—you don't deserve this type of treatment, nobody does and you don't have to accept it! If you allow people to treat you badly now it will lead to unhealthy and potentially abusive relationships when you're older.

Empower yourself now to speak your mind—politely and set boundaries with others you encounter in life. How? It starts with the recognition that your needs, desires and thoughts are just as valuable as everyone else's. Tell people what you want, what you like and what doesn't work for you. Have an opinion and communicate it! As a teen it's not always easy to get parents and teachers to understand your point of view. But it's still important to stay connected to it. Don't just get dragged along by what someone else thinks.

I've studied many of the books written by Jack Canfield (co-author of the *Chicken Soup for the Soul Series*®, *The Success Principles* and others). Jack taught me something wonderful through his *Self-Esteem and Peak Performance* audio tapes. He said, "It doesn't matter what other people do or say to you, it's what you say or do to yourself after they stop talking that's the problem." So if someone puts you down, it's only going to hurt if you agree with them in your head!

Eleanor Roosevelt once said, "No one can make me feel inferior without my consent." So true! If you don't give your power over to someone else, they can't make you feel bad. You control how you feel and respond to things in life. You have a choice, you can be comfortable in all situations, or make yourself uncomfortable and unhappy by taking on what other people are dishing out.

Don't Assume

It's so easy to assume you know what someone else means. But the fact is that most of the time without asking, we might be assuming the wrong thing.

If your mom asks what you're doing you might think it's because she wants you to do something for her (and you don't feel like it at that moment). But it might be because she merely wants to ask you a question that you can quickly answer and get back to what you are doing.

It's a great practice to ask people what they mean when they make a statement. You can use what I call softening statements that make it easier to understand what they want. For instance, you can say:

"Let me ask you a question…"

"That's an interesting question, you must have asked it for a reason."

"I get the feeling that you _____ , is that a fair statement? No, what is then?"

"_____ (person's name), why are you putting all of this pressure on me?"

"I don't understand, can you tell me more about that?"

"There must be a reason you feel that way."

Using some of these softening statements in your daily conversations will help you to understand what your friends, teachers or parents really want. Then you don't have to wonder or assume!

E+R+O

Another concept I learned from Jack Canfield that helped me improve my self-esteem is the formula

E + R + O. The formula says that the events in your life, plus your response to them equal the outcomes you get.

For example: You decide to ask a girl out and she says no. You can be really bummed out and tell yourself how stupid you were for even bothering to humiliate yourself and ask her out. OR you can realize that her saying no has no impact on you personally. She may like someone else or she just may not be attracted to you, which is not a personal reflection on you! We are all entitled to our personal choices so even if you're crazy about her and she's not interested in you—that doesn't mean there is anything wrong with you.

So you can choose to be wounded and sulk about the humiliation of her turning you down, or you can realize that at this time it's not meant to be and move on. Nothing changed, you didn't have a date before you asked her out and aren't any worse off now, right?

The bottom line is you are responsible for everything that happens in your life! You can't blame your parents or teachers or siblings for things that don't go the way you want. Every day you make a conscious choice whether to get upset about something or accept it and move on. It's *your* choice to be happy or sad.

What Are You Good At?

Don't say "nothing" because I don't believe it! You are all here for a reason and every teen out there is good at something. There are five kids in my family. If I think back to the teen years at our house, one sister was great at gymnastics and school, another was a gifted artist and could draw really well, my only brother was a natural athlete, no matter what he tried—he was good at it. Skiing, baseball, football, golf, you name it, he was good at it. My youngest sister was a ham, the entertainer—she could have a room of people laughing in no time. Me? I was a great violinist and singer in my teens, but I sure wasn't a good student, couldn't make the gym team and couldn't draw. Did that make me less than my siblings? No!

Take a few minutes and think about what you're good at. What comes easy to you? What do you enjoy? Get a sheet of paper and make a list of your abilities. And while you're at it, make a list of things you have completed or accomplished so far in life. Yes, you can include being really good at Guitar Hero! Give yourself credit for learning to swim or ride a bike...maybe you too are a gifted athlete or musician?

Making this list will help you see that you have accomplished a lot of things in your life and that you have some special gifts that maybe no one else around you has.

Your Inner Who? That's Crazy!

Another really important aspect to having healthy self-esteem is to stay in touch with your inner child. Can you remember when you were a kid and didn't have the pressures of school, grades, jobs, sports and a ton of extracurricular activities? Can you remember when it felt good to swing as high as you could on the swings? Or maybe the freedom of riding your skateboard up and down the street, skiing, playing hockey, fishing, doing gymnastics, just playing with your friends? Remember the time when you had complete freedom?

For me that time was around five or six years old and I loved to bounce a plastic ball (like you see in the bins at K-Mart) for hours on my grandma's front porch. I had a single aunt who let me watch reruns all day when I visited her because I wasn't allowed to watch much TV at home. Little things that make you giggle with delight because nothing else mattered.

It's important to stay connected with your "inner child" as your grow up. Without the connection to that younger kid in you who knows how to laugh, act silly, have fun and not be self-conscious, you'll become miserable, stiff, appropriate…and dare I say boring!

Learn to be comfortable in your own skin...wherever you are!

Chapter 3

I'm So Stressed, Pressured and Frustrated!

Principle #2 Have Healthy Coping Skills

One thing I've noticed that is vastly different from when I grew up is the pace of life. Today most everyone is living on autopilot. Everyone is "plugged in" all the time. Very rarely are young kids and teens taught to chill out and just be in the moment without being stimulated by a computer, phone, video game, iPod, etc. People have become so attached they don't know how to let go and relax. Don't get me wrong, technology is great. But it needs to have its place.

I was in Hawaii last year to celebrate a special birthday. I was blown away by how many people had their cell phones out at the pool and answered them! The whole point of a vacation is to get away, to let go of all the chores and to-do list from home and to relax.

Down Time

We all need down time. When I talk to adults I talk to them about the importance of taking a time out. Yeah, just the opposite of putting a kid in time out. As you hit your teen years and succumb to all the pressure and demands of your parents, teachers, school, SATs and extracurricular activities you'll join the ranks of many who in their teens are already becoming too familiar with stress. If you don't find a way to deal with it and shut if off you just might find yourself a victim of an addictive behavior. Take your pick: drug addiction, alcoholic, workaholic, super-mom, self-harm, gambling, smoking, eating disorder or maybe morbidly obese. Believe me, you don't want to add this to your list of accomplishments!

Many kids emerge from early childhood with enough baggage that contributes to making them vulnerable to addictions. Without learning any coping skills it can become a lifelong battle.

Causes of Addictions

What are some of the causes of addictions? Depending on your upbringing there may be many factors. I'll list a few here just to give you an idea:

Illustration by Lace Hanson

You don't want to end up like this!

- ✧ Low self-esteem
- ✧ Pressure to be perfect
- ✧ Feeling of not being good enough, not measuring up
- ✧ Sexual abuse
- ✧ Verbal abuse
- ✧ Unhealthy family relationships
- ✧ Not feeling loved, validated or important as a child
- ✧ Poor role models
- ✧ Raised in single parent home without a male or female role model
- ✧ Emotionally sensitive
- ✧ Stress
- ✧ Growing up in poverty

Addiction starts in some people when they take that first sip of alcohol, first hit of pot or heroin, or like me, that first bite of sugar at a time when I was really down. You make the connection between "feeling good" when you smoke, take prescription drugs, gamble or whatever your drug of choice may be. I have studied a great deal about the links between addiction and its causes. I won't wax too scientific or philosophical on you—but want to help you understand that some people really have "addictive personalities" and are more prone to becoming addicted to things. Others are genetically predisposed to addiction because of their family history. That basically means conditions in your body are ripe for addictions; if there is more than one alcoholic in your family your chances for becoming an alcoholic may be escalated.

The reason is that your body responds chemically with a feeling of reward when you indulge. Think about it: when you eat cookies or your favorite junk food—do you want more? Sugar can be just as strong of a chemical addiction as alcohol (which by the way is still sugar). Most kids know that cigarettes are habit forming. That's putting it mildly. Nicotine is very addictive, which is why so many people continue the habit years after they long to quit. Some just give up and don't even try to quit.

Okay, I don't want to nag. If you're like me you're bound to experiment. But be informed; certain drugs and habits are highly addictive. And please don't think you're invincible and can drink and drive! We already have far too many examples of how deadly this combination is for teen drivers.

I Can't Like That!

When my nephew Justin was about two years old, he had a great way of expressing his dissatisfaction with things he didn't like or something he didn't want to do. He would shake his head vigorously and say, "I can't like that!" It still makes me laugh. Sometimes this is exactly what teens need to communicate to others. To say enough is enough.

I recently spoke to a counselor at a high school about the pressures teens face today. We discussed the fact that many teens have no concept of when enough is enough or when to say, "I can't like that." The problem stems from the pressure and expectations of parents. All well intentioned, I'm sure, but parents oftentimes decide or guide their children down the path they feel is "right" for them. "If you take these classes, learn ballet, play football, are active in student senate, go to the same college I did, you'll be successful and a doctor just like me…or a lawyer just like me." After all, the family has three generations of lawyers.

What about what you want? Some kids aren't born to be what their parents want them to be. They feel pressured to live up to Mom and Dad's well-meaning expectations for them and are miserable.

I learned the hard way that there are times you just have to acknowledge you're not cut out for something and let someone else do it. Recently I spent five hours writing up a press release on a book award I received to send to the local media. I kept writing and rewriting, trying to make it more interesting. Now I know I'm not really good at writing press releases but I kept thinking I needed to figure it out. I decided to send it to my editor to proof it for me.

She sent back an email and said, "Lori, this doesn't need to be proofed, it needs to be rewritten." She mentioned she used to write press releases for a living. She offered to do it for me and when I got her copy it was incredible! I made an excuse about why I wasn't good at it and said after twenty-five years of writing business proposals I tend to write factually vs. splashy marketing copy. She said, "Lori, how many hats can you wear?" And with that comment I breathed a huge sigh of relief. I let go of trying to make myself believe that I had to be good at writing in a style that's not comfortable for me.

You can't wear all the hats and be good at EVERYTHING. Even though sometimes it might seem like other kids are good at everything. I guarantee you they aren't.

Here's another example for you. When I got Yager as a puppy, his fur was black, but his undercoat was tan. He is part Malamute, Akita and Husky. I thought, when he was full grown his undercoat would show like a Malamute and his ears would stand up. Well, you can see by his pictures that didn't happen! Ten years later when I got Sasha, a full bred Malamute, her coat was black and white, so naturally I thought as an adult she would black and white. But her coat is just like her mom's (shown in the picture on the next page.)

I think this is sometimes what our parents do. They get this visual of what they think your life should be like and guide you in that direction. It's important to get in touch with what feels right and let go of things that aren't really "you."

Yager the pup

Thought he would look kind of like this

Yager all grown up...looks nothing like the Malamute!

Coping Skills

In order to be successful, happy and live a low-stress life you need to have some coping skills. Things that you can use when you're in the moment of feeling *so* frustrated you are on the verge of acting out. Whether it's screaming something at someone you'll later regret, driving when you're so angry you cause an accident, drinking, smoking a cigarette, or overeating to calm yourself.

Metal of Honor™

I've developed a few tools that can be used when you are at that moment. The first one is called Metal of Honor. I've actually printed this on cards for guys and girls to carry with them and remember to use in times of stress. The intention of this exercise is that you can do it wherever you are, home, school, work, etc. If you are driving—don't close your eyes!

When I'm frustrated or upset and think I can't handle a situation I will remember my Metal of Honor:

M—Meditate, close your eyes, go inside for a minute and FEEL the emotion.

E—Exhale, take 9 slow deep breaths.

T—Tap your abdominals & chest to release the energy. (Make a fist with your hand or hands and tap lightly.)

A—Attitude. Believe in yourself! You can get through this.

L—Let everything be okay.

What this exercise does is helps you move from acting impulsively (being in your head) to responding to the event (E + R + O) from your heart or emotion. It will slow the energy, calm you and help you evaluate the best way to handle the situation. And remember NOTHING is more important than feeling good!

It's very powerful.

Then, at the end of a stressful day, take time to do three things.

1. Journal—Get a special notebook, sit down and write. Just write whatever comes to you. Explore what you are feeling and why you got so revved up over the situation.
2. Nurture—Do something this evening to nurture yourself. Something that makes you feel really good. Read, take a bath or long hot shower, listen to some of your favorite music.
3. Breathe—Spend another 5-10 minutes to sit and breathe deeply. Oxygen is very healing for the body and will make you feel better. Just sit quietly and be in your body.

Don't be afraid to give yourself a time out. Everyone needs to take time to unplug, slow down and connect with what they're feeling. If you get in this habit now as a teen it will serve you well as you experience more stressful situations.

Helping Other People

Another really powerful tool you can use when you are totally stressed out, frustrated and unsure of what's going on is to reach out of your world and help someone else. This tool is very rewarding. First, it takes your mind off of what's driving you crazy, and secondly, you'll be helping someone else and making them feel better.

Who, you ask? Whoever is in need. If you're at school maybe a classmate is having trouble with homework or a situation and you have just the answer they need. If you're at home, maybe taking time to play with a sibling or read to a younger sibling. Maybe one of your parents is having a tough day and by calling him or her to see if there is anything you can do to help, you'll make his day. If you try this one you'll be surprised how much better off you feel. And suddenly you'll find you have the answer or solution to what's been bothering *you*!

Help for Addictions

If you find yourself caught in an addiction that you can't control it's important to find help as soon as you can. Whether it's drugs, alcohol, self-harm, anger, or issues with eating, you can get help. Sometimes the hardest part might be telling your parents. If that seems totally out of the question, try the school counselor or another teacher you trust. Depending on the severity of your addiction you may need to seek out professional help from a treatment center, counselor or someone like me who deals with holistic solutions. Regardless of your situation or location, if you need help you can contact my office and we will help you find a solution. Our number is toll free and confidential 877-650-HEAL.

Chapter 4

⤬

What's on Your Mind?

Principle #3 Know the Power of Your Mindset

What do you spend most of your time thinking about? Dreaming about? Talking about? Watching and listening to? When you wake up in the morning are you happy and looking forward to the day ahead of you or do wake up filled with hatred and resentment?

Your mind is powerful. The thoughts in your mind are a direct link to the results you get in life. I've studied a great deal about the mind. I find it fascinating how we can influence our lives positively or negatively simply by what we focus on. By focus I mean talk about, read, watch, think about, etc.

Your conscious mind does all the thinking and analytical evaluating of situations. It gives the orders much like the captain of a ship. The subconscious mind is the "doer." It doesn't evaluate whether something is good or bad, but it reacts based on the input or order it has been given. What's really cool is that our subconscious thinks in images. Ever hear of a vision board or affirmations? We'll explore those more in a minute.

To further demonstrate how powerful our thoughts are, in the movie *What the Bleep Do We Know!?* Dr. Masaru Emoto found that positive or negative words and phrases typed on paper and affixed to water bottles enacted change in the water's structure. Words like love and gratitude formed beautiful snowflake-like crystals. But negative words had the opposite effect and the water was unable to form crystals. Since our bodies are made up mostly of water this provides a dramatic example of how our thoughts and words affect us. So keeping this in mind, let's explore further how we can positively affect our bodies and world using our thoughts.

F.E.A.R.

Do you know what the word FEAR stands for? False evidence appearing real, or fantasized experience appearing real. Another truly enlightening concept I learned from Jack Canfield. Think about it. When you are scared, what's going through your mind? You are *imagining* a situation you don't want to experience. For example: you're walking down a very dark and quiet street and scared that someone might attack you or kidnap you.

Or maybe you are imagining an experience that you don't think you can handle. Let's say you are scared to see your report card because you're *afraid* of what you grades will be. And if they aren't good, when you go home your parents will yell at you and you'll be grounded. Then you'll miss the dance that you've been looking forward to.

Maybe you've been *afraid* that your girlfriend is going to break up with you. (Perhaps because you don't feel you deserve her.) You worry for two weeks about it and then—it happens!

I'll let you in on a little secret. Life never throws more at us than we can handle. Really! It may not feel that way sometimes when nothing is going right, but it's true. All of these experiences you face every day are here to help you grow and become the wonderful, incredible teenager you were meant to be.

In this way, our mind literally creates our reality—or what happens to us. What if instead of getting caught up in fear and worry you did this:

1. Think about the *worst* possible scenario that could happen as a result of a situation you are afraid of or worried about. Maybe you lied to your teacher and your parents and are afraid you're going to get caught.

2. Accept the worst-case scenario. If this happens, here is how I will deal with it. So if you get caught in the lie, how will you handle it? Can you use this as an opportunity to let your parents and teacher know why you lied? Maybe you need to let them know that you feel they are not listening to you and you don't feel important.

3. Expect the best. After you have identified what you are afraid of or worried about and come to grips with the worst possible scenario of what could happen, *change your focus*! Instead of spending time focused on the bad things that might happen as a result of the worst-case scenario, start to imagine what could happen in the *best*-case scenario. If you explain to your teacher and parents that you don't feel they are listening the situation might improve as a result of this outcome, right?

Athletes manage their thoughts this way all the time. They visualize the outcome they want. I golf a lot and it always makes me laugh when you hear the whack of the club on the ball followed by "Oh man, I *knew* I was going to do that!" That's because in their mind they were so concerned about going in the water the command their subconscious got was "water." And it followed instructions.

It's that simple.

Our Thoughts Create Our Bodies

Our thoughts are so powerful we can literally create and adapt our bodies based on what we think. Example: When I was in fourth grade, I was the first girl to "develop" and wear a bra. The guys in my older sister's class used to make fun of me in the hallway and call me "28 Triple A." I kind of liked the attention but was embarrassed at the same time.

Fast forward to my early forties. As I started to learn more about my body and that our memories are stored not only in our brains but at the cellular level, I had a series of treatments involving deep tissue massage work. One of the treatments was called "letting go." For two nights after that, I could hardly sleep because my arms ached so bad from all the things I had been holding onto for years.

A couple of weeks later I went in for my session and said, "Is it my imagination or have my boobs grown?" My practitioner smiled and told me that is pretty common for women like me who have lived a lot of their life armed with their will and suppressing their emotions. I grew an entire cup size, in my forties!

I call it my organic boob job. That is how powerful our thoughts, embarrassments and beliefs are. We can literally alter physical aspects of our bodies.

Self-Improvement

I've spent many years studying self-improvement. Looking for ways to overcome the insecurities of my teens, improve my self-esteem and live a happier life. In my studies I learned about goal setting and vision boards, which I now do every year on January 1. By setting and achieving goals you can improve your self-confidence and achieve things you want to attain in life. It's always good to have a plan and using goal setting, vision boards and affirmations helps you to solidify the plans you want to follow in your teen years to lead you to the next phase in your life.

What the Heck Are Vision Boards & Affirmations?

A vision board is a visual representation of goals you set for yourself. Things you would like to achieve or have. By combining your goals with visual pictures on a poster board or scrapbook (you can draw them, cut them out of a magazine, etc.), you'll significantly increase your ability to attain that goal.

An affirmation is taking the goal a step further. If you turn your goal into a positive statement that you repeat to yourself morning and night, you'll considerably impact the time it takes to achieve your goal. The key is that your affirmation must be stated as though you have *already achieved* the goal.

Let's look at an example. Say you are interested in trying out for the gym team or football team.

- ✧ First do your research on when the tryouts are and when you have to be ready.
- ✧ Then collect some visual pictures that place you on the gym team or varsity football team that make it feel real.
- ✧ Next create a positive statement something like this: "I am excited to be playing the position of cornerback on the varsity football team in our season opener this year."

Make your affirmation as specific as possible and repeat it for three to five minutes every morning when you first wake up and at night before you go to bed. The timing is very important because early in the morning and late in the evening your conscious mind isn't as alert so it's easier to plug in new images into your subconscious.

This can work for attracting a girl or guy you are interested in. Making better grades, finding a job, improving your grades and more!

Your subconscious mind is driven by visuals, it also like rhymes and rhythm. But it cannot decipher a negative. So don't make an affirmation that says: "I don't want to fail algebra." Instead, state it positively. Maybe like this: "I am so excited with the "B" I got in algebra. My parents are smiling with pride as I show them my grades." Whatever sounds and feels good to you. State it in a way that is real and *feels* good.

Here's another easy yet effective way to help you change your focus and create different results in your life.

1. Make a list of things you *don't* want and be specific (I don't want to be angry all the time, I don't want to have other kids make fun of me, I don't want to eat cookies every time I'm upset).

2. Make a list of what you *do* want and be specific (I want to be happy and enjoy my friends, I want to have lots of new friends, I want to write in my journal when I'm upset and feel better).

3. Feel what it would be like to have what you want—right now! (What does it feel like to enjoy your friends instead of being angry? How would it feel to have true friends that you like to hang out with or play with? To deal with your anger or frustration by journaling or walking the dog? Really feel what this would be like.) Visualize and make up a new story every day about what it feels like to have what you want. Make it *real*.

4. Expect your list of wants to happen. That's it...expect it. Now this is a big although subtle change from knowing it's not going to happen.

These are all fundamentals in what is known as the Universal Law of Attraction, which simply states that what you focus on you will attract—period. If you focus on good things, good things will happen. If you constantly fill your mind with negative, hateful, ugly things you will attract negative experiences into your life. So choose your thoughts, conversations and focus carefully!

Victory Log

Once you start becoming more aware of what you are focusing on and the results it creates in your life you can start a Victory Log. Just a simple list including the date, what happened and how that made you feel. A Victory Log is a wonderful tool to have available when you have to go do something scary or maybe you have to go talk to someone and you're nervous about the conversation. If you read your Victory Log before you do something scary or unsettling it will pump up your confidence and make you feel better about getting it done. Hey, it's all about making life easier, right?

Laughter Is the Best Medicine

It's been said many times—because it's true. Laughter (and oxygen) are very healing and uplifting. If you're having a bad day, find something funny to read, listen to or watch. Call a friend who always makes you laugh and cut loose. Remember to stay in touch with that inner younger child who loves to giggle. What are your favorites? Keep them handy for those days when life just seems unbearable.

Creativity

Are you creative? Everyone is, in one form or another. Exploring the creative things you enjoy doing will go a long way to keeping you happy, healthy and in a good state of mind.

Do you like to play a musical instrument, cook, bake, draw, dance, write stories or lyrics? What are your creative gifts? This doesn't have to be something you do well, just something you like to do that's completely creative. No deadlines, no grades, no judgments…just your personal creations. This is a great life skill that will carry you a long way in feeling good about yourself and appreciating yourself. Even if it's something silly, indulge it. I still like to color with crayons!

I also love to write lyrics, create and sing songs. I'm a great cook and seamstress. All things I learned to do when I was ten years old…and even though for many years I forgot that I *was* creative. When I opened the door and started to exercise the creative muscle again—the creativity came back in avalanches of abundance.

Be Thankful

Here's another thing that's really good for helping you keep your mind focused on positive thoughts. It's very simple. During the day, no matter where you are or what you're doing. Take time out to appreciate people, sights, sounds and events in your life. Be thankful for people, trees, flowers, girls, guys, parents, dogs, cats and smells you get to experience in life. When you are experiencing in a state of gratitude you are living!

And most of all remember nothing is more important than feeling good! Keep your focus, your mind centered throughout the day on things that make you feel good. If you realize that you're getting sucked into negative thoughts or that you're angry and upset, change your thoughts immediately to something that makes you feel good. It will make a big difference in your life!

Chapter 5

⚬⚬⚬

But I Love Fast Food!

Principle #4 Why What You Eat Matters

I thought long and hard about how to share this information with you—because, let's face it: you don't want to hear it. You don't care. When you're a teenager you probably can eat anything you want and not gain weight, right? And you think that as long as you're not overweight you're healthy, right? Maybe not.

Diet and nutrition are the foundation of life. Ever heard someone say, "You are what you eat"? Without the balance of proper nutrients your body and brain cannot function properly. This is why some kids who have really low energy are overweight, crabby or hyperactive. Some teens have really bad acne that can be helped by changing their diet. The problem is most aren't willing to do it.

Combine the lack of a properly balanced diet with an obsession to look like the Jonas Brothers or Miley Cyrus and you now have a problem.

Did you know that 81% of ten year olds are already afraid of being fat? That 77% of young girls surveyed said they would trade their body for that of a celebrity's? That 90% of high school girls diet regularly even though only 10% to 15% are overweight? That 85% of eating disorders start between the ages of thirteen and twenty?

There is a dangerous combination here. A vivid awareness of the images the media is feeding teens of what "perfect" is combined with a poor diet can get you in trouble with weight issues and eating disorders, which we've already touched on. The risk is far greater than it seems when it first starts. By doing things like skipping meals and living on soda, coffee, pizza, ice cream and hamburgers, your body doesn't get the nutrition it needs, which results in depleted chemicals that feed your brain.

Brain Chemistry

Your brain needs a balance of amino acids to function properly. Without them you can end up depressed, blah, stressed out and overly sensitive. What happens next? Most people head to the doctor's office to find out what's wrong. The doctor oftentimes give a prescription and now you have a band aid to cover up a symptom that's caused by a poor diet and lack of nutrition.

Sugar

Let's talk about sugar. Did you know that in the 18th century Americans only consumed an average of seven pounds of sugar a year? Check out this:

Sugar Consumption in United States

18th century =   7 pounds per year
19th century = 52 pounds per year
20th century = 150 pounds per year

Source: New England Primer

Sugar consumption has skyrocketed! The problem is sugar is hidden in many foods you eat.

If you exist on mainly fast food, and what I call "white foods," including pizza, pasta, bagels, white breads, ice cream, donuts, etc., you're getting a ton a sugar in everything you eat. Then you wake up the next day and you want more! For some kids the issues will emerge early. Gaining weight as a child may lead to a painful existence that continues for many years until they decide to step out of their comfort zone and make a change to improve their health.

Yeah, so you're young and it doesn't matter, right? Do you get sick a lot? Colds and flu every time they are going around? It's because your immune system is beat down and can't combat the illness because it is weakened by all the sugar you consume.

Sugar contributes to hyperactivity in kids, difficulty concentrating, crankiness, diabetes, and can lead to cancer, migraine headaches, food allergies, ulcers and of course obesity. This is actually a very small list of all the conditions sugar contributes to.

Caffeine and Soda Pop

I don't suppose you've ever heard that caffeine, alcohol, and soda pop aren't good for you? Caffeine is a stimulant and is another addictive substance. Alcohol and soda are all sugar and what we call empty calories, no nutritional value for our bodies. If you already drink lots of pop, or drink soda with every meal this will be another continuing habit you'll have to deal with later in life.

If you're going to drink soda be sure to include water as part of your daily intake. Since our bodies are mostly water we need to drink water to keep our insides running smoothly.

But I Hate Vegetables!

The best diet for you is eating three balanced meals a day with one to two healthy snacks in between. Balanced meals include a serving of healthy protein (chicken, fish, lean red meat) with a serving of carbohydrates (wheat bread, brown rice, fruit) at every meal. At least two meals a day should include fresh vegetables. And most importantly you need at least one green leafy vegetable a day. Before you say yuck—what if I told you the greens would improve your ability to concentrate, your focus and overall health? Something to think about. Greens include broccoli, green beans, Brussels sprouts, kale, mustard greens, spinach, romaine lettuce, etc.

The less processed food (such as frozen, from a box, fast food) you eat and the more fresh food you eat the better. Include a variety of fresh fruits and vegetables—your body will thank you.

Healthy Snacks

I actually believe our bodies do better when we don't go any longer than three to four hours without eating. In-between meal snacks can include raisins, almonds, walnuts, celery with peanut butter or almond butter, fresh fruit. You have lots of options without hitting the sugary or frozen options.

One way you can help your parents is to plan your lunch and snacks ahead. Yeah, you probably like to eat the junk you get at school. But if you would like to have more energy and nicer skin and more focus try one or two suggestions from this chapter and see if you don't feel better. Four principles down, one to go.

Chapter 6

Centered, Balanced & Grounded?

Principle #5 Improve Physical & Mental Health

Have you ever thought about what having balance in your life means? No, it's not being able to stand on a stool or tall ladder with one foot! You've probably heard people talk about being off-kilter, out of balance or, my favorite term, discombobulated. What about being grounded and centered? In order to really thrive in life you need to have everything in balance, all three dimensions: mind, body and spirit.

If you approach everything by sheer force of willpower and control to make them happen the way you want, you won't be very happy with the results. But if you are open to watching for the paths or guidance that comes your way—little signals that *this* is the right thing to do or *that* is the wrong thing to do—your life will be much easier. I call it my "gut" instinct.

Have you ever gotten ready to go somewhere and had the feeling you should take your umbrella, or maybe you shouldn't wear the shoes you have on? Or maybe wear jeans instead of shorts. And, when you got there, you realized you should have trusted your gut because it did rain and you were cold in shorts? That's called intuition. That "inner knowing" about something. Everyone has it and if you tune in to it and exercise your "gut feelings" they will get stronger and will always guide you

It's the same with mental and physical health. You need exercise to keep both your mind and body balanced. Some forms of exercise are obvious; others might be new to you. Your body needs fresh air and multiple forms of exercise to maintain balance and thrive. Here are a few ideas you can incorporate into your daily or weekly routine.

Sunshine

Get plenty of fresh air and sunshine. Our bodies thrive on oxygen from fresh air and good old-fashioned sunlight. If you're always inside and any exercise you do is inside, break up the pace by going for a walk two or three times a week. Take the dog for a walk to the park, play in the snow, or swim in the ocean—use whatever form of fresh air is in your backyard.

You Gotta Move!

Being sedentary as a teen just isn't natural. At your age you should have plenty of energy to play sports and get some exercise. Your body will benefit from aerobics, which is good for the heart (running, riding your bicycle, swimming, jumping rope, playing soccer, football, basketball, hockey—anything to get your heart pumping) and resistance exercises...

Resistance Training

Resistance isn't defined as "No, I don't want to do that." It usually involves working out with weights, or large rubber bands, a large ball, etc. Something that will offer resistance and helps build and tone your muscles. Weight training is great for girls too. You don't have to get ripped (really defined, like a body builder) to lift weights. It will improve your strength and give you strong bones, which is important as you get a little older. Pilates is also good for overall conditioning.

Moving Your Energy

In addition to cardio and strength training are various forms of exercise including energy movement. Tai Chi, Tae Kwon Do, Karate and Yoga are examples. They involve more concentration and more of an emotional connection versus aerobics and strength training, which involve your will or willpower.

Did you know everyone and everything is energy? Sometimes you develop energy blocks just like a mental block. When this happens you don't function properly. There may even be some form of physical discomfort associated with having an energy block.

Being unable to let go of discouraging incidents that happen to you or comments someone said to you will contribute to the amount of stress you carry and subsequently to your level of physical health. This is why different forms of exercise and learning to move your energy are so powerful.

Quiet Time

To improve your mental health, give your brain time to slow down, time to do nothing. This isn't the same as sleep, although you certainly need a lot of that as a teenager. For teens having the time to just sit and be still is desperately lacking these days. Are you ever in a place where you aren't listening to music, watching TV, on the computer, on your cell phone or talking to someone? Your brain and body need an occasional time out.

Taking a time out involves taking a few minutes to just sit quietly with your eyes closed and tuning in to what's going on inside of you. What are you feeling physically? Are you stressed, tense or relaxed? What are your thoughts focused on? Can you slow them down by taking a few deep breaths? Where is your breathing coming from—low in your belly or up higher in your chest? What sensations are in your body?

Take a few minutes and listen to what your intuition is telling you. Get connected to your authentic or true self. Just like the Metal of Honor exercise, spending a few minutes a day to quiet yourself is very calming for the brain and will help you eliminate stress and even sleep better! I call it meditation, but some people have a problem with that title, so call it quiet time or whatever you like. It's all the same!

You're Grounded

To be grounded means you are energetically connected with Mother Earth. It's important even as teens to stay connected, centered and grounded. What does that mean? It means thinking before you act, not getting so excited that you do something totally stupid you knew you would get in trouble for (sneaking off school campus with other kids, driving drunk, pulling a *really* mean prank on another kid, getting pregnant). It means not forgetting your chores when it was something that was really important to your mom or dad. It means thinking of other people in addition to yourself, realizing that it isn't all about you. Being grounded helps you live more from your heart than impulsively from your head.

Dealing with Other People's Energy

In life you will encounter four types of energy. Push, Pull, Stop and Allow. You have a choice in how you respond to each type of energy, just like the $E = R = O$ formula we talked about before. How you respond to be pushed, pulled or blocked by other people equates to the amount of energy you expend and sometimes waste on that person—or their energy.

Push

Push energy is like when you're walking down the hallway at school and you can feel someone behind you who can't wait to get past and is pushing you to walk faster. The choice you have is to either get frustrated and purposely slow down or stop (and piss them off) or simply choose to allow them to go around you (which means in effect you are pushing their energy beyond you and allowing it to go right over or around you).

Pull

Pull energy is that guy or girl you know that wears you out. Every time you're with this person you leave feeling totally drained like they are sucking the life out of you! It may even be your boyfriend or girlfriend. It could be a chronic complainer, or a kid who's always doing or saying mean things.

Again, you have a choice of how to respond to this type of person. Instead of letting them suck the life out of you and wear you out, you can decide not to spend time with this person. You may decide to find different friends, people with more positive energy where you enjoy their company and they enjoy yours. There isn't a strain (push or pull) in your interactions.

So how do you let go of a energy puller? That can be difficult initially. They will be persistent because they love the energy they get from you. They may continue to call and text you and post things on your MySpace page. You can be polite and still exit yourself from the relationship.

<u>Stop</u>

Stop energy is the person (maybe a teacher or parent) who you just can't seem to connect with no matter how hard you try. They say *day*, you say *night*, they say *wrong*, you say *right*. You feel like you're up against a brick wall when you deal with them. It can be incredibly frustrating, if you let it. Again you make the choice how you respond to this type of person.

You can push them, or try to pull from them but you probably won't get too far. Maybe you can just go around them. Most likely you can find other ways to get what you need. If it's a parent, sibling or teacher—someone you interact with regularly who has significant influence in your life it—might be worth asking them how you can communicate more effectively. Be proactive and ask if there is another way you can present information to them that will make it easier for them to respond to.

We each have different input and output modes for how we process information. You may notice that some people are more visual—they always want to read a book, or have a print out rather than reading online. They describe thing by using words like "I see."

Other people are more auditory—I always notice the waiters who don't need to write down a table full of orders whether you add pickles, hold the mustard, or add extra mayo. I can't do that—I have to write it down! Theses people describe things by using words like "I hear you."

The third category is people who are kinesthetic—people who learn by doing and by feel. Kids who love to dance are typically very kinesthetic. The kid who always touches your arm when he or she passes by and asks you how you "feel" is generally more kinesthetic.

By understanding people's input and output modes you can affect your interactions with them. It's also important to know that some people take input in one mode (visual) and give output in a different mode (auditory).

Allow

Allow energy is a person or people you get along with. The best friend who *always* knows what you're thinking, can finish your sentences and always has your back. Everything is easy when you encounter allow energy…it isn't work. It feels natural, safe and wonderful. Unfortunately everyone you meet won't be sharing this type of energy with you.

Understanding a little about the energy that surrounds you will help you decide who you want to be your friend and spend your time with. It will help you determine who has your best interest at heart and who you are better off not associating with. It will help you be more conscious, more aware.

Live in the Moment

The objective of becoming more conscious is to help you learn how to live fully in this moment. To enjoy each and every day to its fullest. When you're a teen sometimes it seems like certain days or weeks you're looking forward to will never arrive. You spend a lot of time focused on that special occasion or date and tune out what's happening around you today. The more conscious you become the better choices you will make.

One thing that will help you become more conscious is taking time to be reflective, time where you aren't listening, talking or doing. Taking time to think about the events of the day, what happened and why they happened the way they did will increase your awareness. This is where journaling is also quite helpful. Another way to learn how to be in the moment vs. simply reacting is using the technique of being The Witness.

The Witness

There's a process I learned from one of my mentors, Bill Harris. Bill describes the process of being the Witness as a way to become more conscious or more aware of things you're doing. To be the witness, you watch a situation or behavior as if you are a third party (or an audience) even though you are in the situation. You note every detail carefully as if you were a scientist. What triggered the situation? What is happening as a result of your response to the situation? What can you learn by watching the response and interaction of the people involved in the situation?

Here's an example. Let's say you keep getting in trouble at school. You're in trouble because you keep causing disturbances in class. If you have a desire to change your behavior and don't really want to continue getting in trouble you can decide that next time it happens you are going to take mental notes of how it happens to see what you can learn from it.

The next day you're in class and all of a sudden, with your awareness motor in full swing, you realize that you are throwing paper at the cute girl you like, texting when your phone is supposed to be off and, oh crap!, here comes the teacher and you're in trouble again. But this time you made a mental note of what happened. You didn't understand what the teacher was talking about and got bored. To hide your inability to comprehend and cover in case the teacher called on you for an answer you started acting out.

Continue on to the principal's office. You notice your attitude and how you lip off to the principal. You notice how you slump in the chair like you don't care about anyone or anything and you listen as you cuss the teacher out for giving you more detention, which results in extended time.

You get the idea. You can apply it to anything. Once you are aware, it's a lot easier to change a behavior that isn't productive or always getting you in trouble. Now the next time it happens you'll be in witness mode again and if you're ready can change your thought process and response to the events. Remember nothing in life is more important than feeling good.

Self–healing

Believe it or not we all come pre-wired to heal ourselves. We all possess the knowledge we need to make ourselves better and well. Sometimes accessing that information is more difficult than at other times. In American society people have come to expect that there is a pill for everything. But the answer to most ailments lies in the body itself. Through a combination of using the subconscious and Eastern medicine techniques like acupuncture and energy healing, many teens have been led to their own self-healing.

Now I realize many of you may not have the chance or opportunity to explore alternative methods of healing (and you may face push back from your parents), but there are many natural remedies that don't include popping any pills that are very effective and have been around for years. If not now, as you get older you can explore the alternatives.

SWET'N

I created a little acronym to remind you what you need in order to be balanced, centered and grounded. Ready?

S —You need adequate sleep every night
W—You need to drink plenty of water
(typically 6-8 glasses a day)
E —You need regular exercise (aerobic,
strength and energy)
T —You've got to take a time out and find
quiet time on a weekly basis
N —You need a balanced healthy nutrition
plan

Remember to nurture yourself on occasion! Do something fun that makes you feel really good. Ask your parents to rent a special movie you'd like to watch. Or to take you to a new movie that's coming out or to your favorite store.

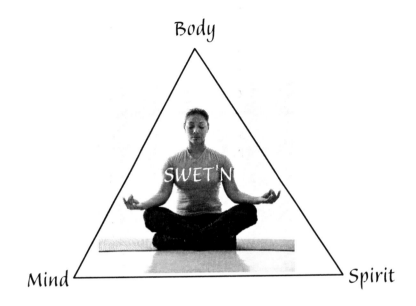

NOTHING is more important than feeling good!

Chapter Seven

Things I Wish I Knew
Then—That I Know Now

Now I don't want you to think I've lived a life full of regrets...far from it. Although as I mentioned, there are a few things I would have changed as a teenager. Guess we can all say that! I do want to share a few thoughts about things I really wish I had known in my teens. Hopefully one or two of them will be helpful for you as you continue on the path through adolescence to an adult.

You Can Do **<u>ANYTHING</u>** You Set Your Mind to

I wish I'd known that you can have, do or be anything you want. There are no limits. Whatever you conceptualize in your brain, decide you want, visualize and believe firmly in, you can have. I spent so much of my life drenched in all the reasons I couldn't do something or couldn't have things I wanted badly. As I learned about the power of the subconscious, began to set and achieve goals I was blown away that I didn't know this before.

Many athletes are tuned into visualization and practice through mental images. Three of my favorites are Andre Agassi (tennis), Tiger Woods (golf) and Michael Jordan (basketball). I love watching tennis and specifically Andre after his comeback. Watching him get two sets down and suddenly get the determination in his eye that he could outlast the opponent and win the match was awesome!

Tiger Woods is incredible. Words can't do justice in describing the concentration and drive he has to compete and win. He's done some phenomenal things in his career, most recently winning a tournament in 2008 in a playoff on Monday while grimacing in pain with a torn ligament. Then winning in his third tournament back the next year. Tiger has a level of mental focus that to me demonstrates the true power of focus and belief in yourself.

Then there is Michael Jordan. Most of you probably never saw him play in the early nineties but he also was phenomenal. (I love sports, by the way.) His drive to exceed and succeed were unmatched, scoring double digit points on a night when he had the flu. And the number of games he had with triple-doubles! Amazing.

Think about these guys next time you want

something badly. They exemplify the power of focus and what having belief in yourself can do.

~~Can't~~

If there is one word I could strike from the English language it would be this one. The only reason you can't do something is because you tell yourself you can't and you believe you can't. If you change your dialogue and start talking not only about can do, but already having done the thing, the impact will astound you. So give it a shot. Remove can't from your vocabulary.

~~Try~~

A close second is the word try. Ever have someone tell you they will try to come by your party or event? Do they show? No. Whenever you are talking to someone who says they will try to come by your house, or your party, or will try to call you, don't count on it. It means you're only penciled in and if something more important comes along you won't see them.

Etiquette

As far as I can tell etiquette for the most part has gone out the window. I keep saying I'm going to write a book about cell phone etiquette and it's still needed. Because everyone has to be on the phone constantly, people are in training to be rude. All the time I see people checking out at a store and not even acknowledging the clerk who is ringing up their order because they are too engrossed in their conversation.

Chivalry isn't dead. Guys: girls still like to have you help them put their coat on. They still like you to open the car door for them. What ever happened to manners? It's just downright rude to let the door slam in someone else's face. So hold the door open for the little old lady (or man). Help another student pick up the books they dropped without making them feel stupid.

Be polite, say please and thank you. It's not hard to do and, like everything else, will come back to you. The more you appreciate, the more you'll receive.

Everything Is Negotiable

Seriously! You don't lose anything by asking and many times you'll get a better seat, better price or better understanding of something by asking. Approaching life with the knowledge that all things are negotiable keeps you aware and on your toes. You will be prepared when someone makes a move to take the upper hand (or paw) in a situation.

The "art" of negotiation

Relationships, Yours, Mine, Ours

There are a few things I wish I had understood about dating and relationships in my teens that I didn't have a clue about.

The first one is, if a guy or girl breaks off a date or breaks up with you just let it go. It isn't a personal reflection on you, even if they don't like you any more. This is a free country and whom you date is a choice. Haven't you ever been in a relationship or a friendship that over time you just grew out of? It doesn't mean there was anything wrong with that person—there was just a shift.

Secondly, I learned that you don't always have to have "closure" after a break up. In your teens everyone is fickle. One day someone might like you, the next day they might not. It isn't the end of the world! Just let it go. Move on. Next? And by the way, you won't attract the next person when you are still crying over the previous one. You have to let go to be able to attract the energy of a new girlfriend or boyfriend.

Third, don't emulate cling wrap. I sincerely feel for the guys I dated when I was an insecure teenager. I wanted and needed acceptance so badly and thought I was supposed to get it from guys. I can only imagine how clingy I was.

No one owns anyone else. If you're with some-one, trust him or her; if you don't, let him go. All the girls and guys with a jealous streak who feel they have to constantly check up on their boyfriend or girlfriend are only waving their bright red flag of insecurities for all to see.

If you become sexually active as a teen, know the risks. It's far easier to get pregnant than most kids realize. Add sexually transmitted diseases to the mix and for most kids it probably makes sense to wait awhile, until you're in a committed relationship and don't have to sneak around. While guys are experimenting and often just collecting experiences, girls are looking for love and validation through sex. It's a completely different experience for both. It can lead to a lot of fear (about pregnancy and disease) and hurt if you get dumped after "doing" somebody.

Lastly, I learned you can't control or change other people. The sooner you figure this one out the easier life will be. You'll meet people along the way who will try to change and control you. It's usually not a lot of fun. Just realize they are not comfortable with who they are and let them go, because you can't change them either. No matter how gorgeous he or she is.

A Reason, a Season or a Lifetime

Sometimes it's difficult to understand where you stand with a friend. Why they act friendly one day and like they don't know you the next. For me friendships in my teens were not easy. I didn't feel like I fit in, didn't feel like most people liked me and didn't understand how I could change the situation or even why I had to.

It seems that teens either have solid best friends that they hang out with all the time or their friends change regularly like a revolving door because kids are ruled by peer pressure. Sometimes so-called friends ignore you when they are with others because of that peer pressure too. It sounds really hurtful but it's all too common.

As much as it's important as a teen to fit in and be a part of the group, as I've mentioned before, it is perfectly fine to be yourself, be comfortable with yourself and not succumb to peer pressure or the fickle games that guys and girls play.

I still think about an email I received a long time ago about friends. In essence this is what it said:

Some friends come in for a reason. The friendship may not last long, but by that association you will be enlightened or have an experience that you need as you continue through life.

Some friends come into your life for a season. Maybe you are best friends with someone for a year and they move away. Or maybe you are dating someone for the summer and then you break up.

These people are in your life for a "season" or period of time. Again, it's best just to enjoy the time you had instead of wondering why they went away.

Lastly, some friends you will have for a lifetime. (BFF's, best friends forever). These are special relationships and their purpose is different than with those we only have a limited amount of time with. These are the people you can count on to always "have your back" and be there for you. Cherish these friends—they are truly special!

Depression, Suicide and Trauma

Some teens get so overwhelmed with life they become depressed and may even start to have suicidal thoughts. If you or someone you know begins to experience these types of emotions, this is serious stuff. Do something about it. Many teen suicides and shooting rampages could be avoided if the kids who are around that person took his or her words and actions seriously. It's hard to think the other person might actually follow through with what he is saying, but it's a lot better to be proactive and save lives than to wake up one morning and find out someone you know committed suicide. Or someone brings a gun to school and takes out his problems on teachers and students after warning he was going to do it. Sadly, we know from hindsight that these kids leave clues.

Diversity

Consider this: we're all on this planet to further expand our capacity to love. To learn how to accept people who aren't exactly like us. We are blessed to live in a society where we have lots of cultures and colors. Embrace the diversity! It brings great variety to life. Don't make fun of kids who have an accent or who dress differently than you. Different doesn't mean sub-standard or unworthy. It's just different. Some people like apples and some prefer oranges.

Crying

This is always an interesting topic. We're all raised to believe that if a boy cries he's a crybaby and that girls cry to get what they want. It's sad because we need to be in touch with and express our emotions. But it's also important to know when to control them—yeah the pressures of society. There is nothing worse than being made fun of when you are crying! Well, I suppose there is, but it's humiliating and makes you feel even worse. The best advice I can give you is that it *is* important to express your emotions and if you are hurting, let someone know. Also, try journaling—it's a great way to help you stay in touch with what's going on and how you're feeling. It will help you learn how to process events and situations that make you feel vulnerable. But don't forget, a good cry when you're all alone can be a great way to let off steam.

Reach Out—Be Friendly

Ever go to a party where you don't know a lot of people? It's painful if you're too shy to figure out how to start a conversation and blend in. One piece of advice I learned in sales that I wish I had known as a kid makes it so much easier. Whenever you go to a party or school or purely social event remember that everyone else there is probably just as uncomfortable as you are.

Approach people who are in groups of two, or perhaps someone standing alone. Ask them how they know the host or how they were invited to the event. To keep the conversation going ask what their favorite YouTube video or movie is. You'll probably see a huge sigh of relief on the other person's face as you've just made them more comfortable in asking about them. In return you're no longer standing or sitting alone feeling like a dork or loser because you don't know anyone.

Love and Accept Yourself

This is a big one. If you don't truly appreciate, accept and love yourself, take the necessary steps to increase your self-esteem while you're young. What other people think about you or say about you is none of your business. It shouldn't affect you at all if you are comfortable with whom you are. That's the goal. Think of all the celebrities who see all the lies printed about them in the tabloids every week. If they let everything in print bother them they would be a mess.

Don't Be Afraid to Be Unique

Teens aren't all cut from the same mold. Some are more eccentric than others. Some are more nerdy. Some are prettier. Everyone has their purpose.

There is room for everyone to fit into this puzzle called teen life. No need to stress about fitting in and why you're different. One day soon you'll know why and love it.

Follow Your Heart

Speaking of your life's purpose...don't forget to follow your heart. If you're feeling pressure to pursue classes you don't want to or extracurricular activities that you don't really enjoy, talk to your parents or teachers. Negotiate with them. Explain why this just isn't a fit and what it is you *do* want to do. Honor your gut, it will reward you.

Look for the Lesson

The best thing about life that many teens miss is that there is always a lesson in everything that happens. If your true love just dumped you, or you didn't get the role you wanted in the school play, be open to learning what the lesson was you were supposed to learn. As trite as it sounds, when one door closes another one opens. It's true! I think oftentimes kids (and some adults) miss the open door because their eyes are glued to the one that's shut and are trying to figure out how to gain entrance back in. Even if you're in a car accident or something that feels equally as bad, look for the lesson. What are you supposed to learn from it? Then be ready to move on.

Visualize Your Dreams

We've already talked about the how. But realize that even as a teenager you can begin to focus on and visualize your dreams and goals. What are they? Do you want to own your own beauty salon, be the first female president of the United States, play quarterback for Notre Dame or be an all-star forward in the NBA? Start now to attract what you desire.

Don't Worry, Be Happy

This is the title of a great song written by Bobby McFerrin. Great advice for everyday life, don't worry, be happy. Treat other people as you'd like them to treat you. Talk about other people like you'd like them to talk about you. And remember nothing is more important than feeling good!

You can do more than survive; you can THRIVE in your teens. It's all up to you, it's your choice.

Bonus Chapter

Life Lessons from Sasha

D o you blog? Between my blogs and news-letters I include stories of life lessons from Sasha's perspective. By now you have figured out that I love animals and specifically my two dogs. So I thought I would share a few here that may be of interest and amusement to you.

Stepping Out of Your Comfort Zone

Sasha and Yager have been actively helping me prepare for my upcoming speeches. They continue to act out scenarios that give me great analogies for life.

Sasha loves water. Not just a little bit, she LOVES water. Recently when I was taking a relaxing bubble bath she was quite intrigued. So I tried to get her to jump in the tub (don't worry I would have been out by that time!) She wanted to get in so badly but was unsure how to take that first step over the edge of the tub. Yager kept coming over to see what was going on. She got so distracted by pushing him out of the way that she kept missing her opportunity to play in the water. Every time she thought about giving it a try and getting her nerve up, Yager came around and she immediately put a blocking move on him. It was quite comical to watch.

Much like life, she was apprehensive about trying something new and stepping out of her comfort zone. In the process of thinking about how she would approach this new thing she continually let herself get distracted by Yager, who was merely watching. She continued to be so concerned about him vs. pushing herself to take the step forward and get the reward for taking the risk of jumping over the side of the tub. A reward that would have delighted her immensely. She lost focus and was more concerned about what somebody else thought than just doing her own thing. She missed a great opportunity.

Feeling Stuck?

Sasha has found a new past time. She has discovered that she can see out the window (in front of the house) and watch the world go by from the guest room upstairs. This new discovery gives her a whole new vantage point to view the world. At times she races up and down the stairs to check out the window and then runs outside to investigate further. The window was there all the time, but she just discovered this vantage point in the past month. She's found a whole new way to view the world from her existing situation.

This scenario makes me think about how we often feel stuck in a situation and can't see a way out. Sometimes just by adjusting our thinking, by being open to new ways to view a situation we are led to the answer that is right in front of us. It may not even require any money. For example, even in this so-called "bad" economy we can all thrive. What if you adjusted your focus, words and thoughts to that of prosperity instead of spending time in worry and fear about all the potentially bad things that might happen with the economy? Is there a situation you're feeling stuck in? Follow Sasha's lead and look for the new way to view it!

Staying in Touch With Your Inner Puppy (aka Child)

Sasha is working hard to stay in touch with her inner child "aka puppy." The importance of which I've talked a lot about with the holidays.

She will be two in February and is starting to mellow a little bit. (Hurray!) But there is one thing that keeps her inner puppy alive and well.

Each week after we shop at the farmer's market we head to the doggie park. Now that it's been a ritual for her and big brother Yager to ride along for the past seven to eight months she knows the routine. As we roll closer to our destination and get within ¾ of a mile from the park she explodes with excitement and bounces excitedly from left window to right window with anticipation in the back of the SUV. Once inside the gate she (and Yag) run as fast as they can to greet their buddies. Her favorite thing at the dog park is finding the one dog who is willing to run and the chase ensues. (She was one of twelve puppies so playing chase with a pack of dogs brings back fond puppyhood memories.)

Sasha shows up as it's time to leave. As we exit the gate and she takes one last look at her friends her pace begins to slow. On occasion she will even stop and sit about fifty feet from the car in silent protest for a moment as she would prefer to stay all day. She knows its important to take time out to play, get some exercise and enjoy friends. How about you? What's the thing that gets you excited or makes you giggle with delight? (The golf course always does the trick for me—no surprise there!) Remember to schedule time to connect and play with your inner child! It'll keep ya young!

Be Persistent

Persistence is a great attribute to possess. And Sasha has learned from the best. Well, okay, it was built in there somewhere!

I had a great laugh the other day when she had been trying to get me up from the computer to come and play for awhile. First she brought the octopus, which has no stuffing (she loves to play tug of war). Then it was the little round toy made from rope. Next? Her football, then her basketball, which she loves to squeak. When I finished the task at hand and got up to play there was a neat little trail of all the toys she used to try and bait me to play. It was hysterical, this line of toys up to the office door.

Her persistence paid off. It wasn't that I hadn't wanted to play, but it had to be the right time—once I was done with my project. It's the same in life. Often when we hear "no" or get no response at all, it doesn't mean the answer won't be yes...when the timing is right. So be persistent, ask for what you want and don't give up!

Ask for What You Want

Sasha has started a new ritual in the past month. Anytime I get ready to leave the house she races me down to the first landing on my stairs and quickly lies down on her back begging for a belly rub. Once I oblige her she jumps up and races to a spot right in front of my office and again lies down and insists on another belly rub. It's hysterical! She's created a toll system where I'm asked to pay toll in order to pass by and leave the house.

The moral of the story...Sasha says: "Always ask for what you want. You can't get what you want from someone if you don't ask for it—and sometimes you'll get exactly what you were hoping for!"

Remember to Take a Breather

As I finish up my monthly newsletter my office assistant, Sasha is fast asleep on the floor beside me.

She's very good at making sure I don't work too long without a break. Every day at 4 p.m., she walks in front of the keyboard tray on my credenza and pushes it away so I can't type. Her signal that it's time for the afternoon stretch! If I don't respond in a timely manner, she ever so politely lays her 65 pounds across my lap! It's like having a personalized time clock.

Resources for Teens

Online Resources

Teen Line: http://TeenlineOnline.org

> TEEN LINE was founded in 1980 to help adolescents address their problems through a confidential peer hotline and community outreach program. It is operated by TEENS for teens

Institute for Girls Development:
http://www.InstituteForGirlsDevelopment.com

> The Institute for Girls' Development is dedicated to empowering girls. We offer caring, comprehensive, and innovative programs and services for girls, their families, and their circles or community.

Learn2Balance: http://www.Learn2Balance.com

> Holistic solutions for eating disorders and life. Resources and Information on eating disorders, weight and stress management.

National Eating Disorder Association:
http://www.NationalEatingDisorders.org

> Our organization is dedicated to providing education, resources and support to those affected by eating disorders.

Check Yourself Hotlines & Help:
http://www.checkyourself.org/Hotlines.aspx

> Info for drug and alcohol treatment, runaways, depression, abuse, rape and incest, gay and lesbian, HIV and AIDS and Sex.

Check for regular updates on www.Learn2Balance.com

Recommended Books/Audio Series

Many of the authors listed here have multiple books and audio series available on their websites. I've just listed a few here.

Jack Canfield, www.jackcanfield.com
- ✧ *The Success Principles, The Power of Focus, The Aladdin Factor*

Dr. Wayne Dyer, www.drwaynedyer.com
- ✧ *The Power Of Intention, Being in Balance*

Lynn Grabhorn, www.lynngrabhorn.com
- ✧ *Excuse Me Your Life is Waiting*

Esther and Daniel Hicks, www.abraham-hicks.com
- ✧ *Ask and It Is Given: Learning to Manifest Your Desires*

Bill Harris, www.amazon.com
- ✧ *Thresholds of the Mind*

Napoleon Hill, W. Clement Stone www.amazon.com
 ✧ *Success Through A Positive Mental Attitude,*
Napoleon Hill, www.amazon.com
 ✧ *Keys to Success: The 17 Principles of Personal Achievement*
Bill Phillips and Phil D'Orso, www.bodyforlife.com
 ✧ *Body—for—Life, 12 Weeks to Mental and Physical Strength*
Julia Ross, www.themoodcure.com
 ✧ *The Mood Cure*
Brian Tracy, www.briantracy.com
 ✧ *The Psychology of Achievement, The Science of Self-Confidence*

Index

Did You Borrow This Copy?

To order this book by
Shewolf Press

Online orders:
www.ShewolfPress.com

E-mail:
Lori@Learn2Balance.com

Postal orders:
Shewolf Press
25379 Wayne Mills Pl. #228
Valencia, CA 91355
661-670-0729

Please send [   ] copies of *Teen Secrets to Surviving & THRIVING* @ $12.95

Shipping and handling: $5.00 for the first book and $1.00 for each additional

Payment: Certified check or money order

Total $ _____

Name: _____
Address: _____
City: _____ State: _____ Zip: _____
Telephone: _____
E-mail address: _____

Wholesale discounts available on large quantities.

Thank you!